Contents

Apollo 13

Adapted from the junior
novelization by
DINA ANASTASIO
Based on the motion picture screenplay
written by
WILLIAM BROYLES, JR. &
AL REINERT, and JOHN SAYLES
Based on the book *Lost Moon* by
JIM LOVELL and JEFFREY
KLUGER

Level 2

Retold by Brent Furnas
Series Editors: Andy Hopkins and Jocelyn Potter

Pearson Education Limited
Edinburgh Gate, Harlow,
Essex CM20 2JE, England
and Associated Companies throughout the world.

ISBN 0 582 451841

First published in the UK in 1995 by Sapling, an imprint of Boxtree Limited, London.
First published in the USA in 1995 by Grosset & Dunlap, Inc.,
a member of The Putnam & Grosset Group, New York.
This edition first published 2001

Typeset by Pantek Arts Ltd, Maidstone, Kent
Set in 11/14 pt Bembo
Printed and bound in Denmark by Norhaven A/S, Vibrog

Published by Pearson Education Limited in association with
Penguin Books Ltd, both companies being subsidiaries of Pearson Plc

For a complete list of the titles available in the Penguin Readers series please write to your local
Pearson Education office or to: Marketing Department, Penguin Longman Publishing,
5 Bentinck Street, London, W1M 5RN.

Introduction

Suddenly, there was a loud noise and Jim flew into a wall.

"WHAT WAS THAT?" he shouted.

Jack sat in his chair and watched papers and bags of food fly around inside the command module.

"What happened?" Jim asked again. He looked at the other astronauts, but they didn't answer.

Then there was a second noise.

"Look!" said Fred. "The lights on the controls are going crazy! I never saw that before!"

Jack spoke into the radio. "Houston, we have a problem."

It is Monday, April 13, 1970 and *Apollo 13* is flying through space. The three astronauts in the command module are going to the Moon. Suddenly, something goes wrong. There is a loud noise and the command module loses power. Oxygen is leaving the ship. The astronauts can't live without oxygen or power. What can they do? What can their controllers in Houston do? Will the astronauts walk on the Moon? Will they get home again?

Jim Lovell and Jeffrey Kluger wrote a book about this trip, *Lost Moon*. Then, William Broyles, Al Reinert, and John Sayles turned the book into the great movie, *Apollo 13*, with Tom Hanks. This Penguin Reader comes from Dina Anastasio's story of the movie.

Neil Armstrong was the first man on the Moon.

Chapter 1   July 20, 1969

The lunar module was on the Moon. Astronaut Neil Armstrong came out of the door and looked up into black space. He looked down at the gray rocks. The Moon waited. Slowly, he moved down the stairs. When he got to the bottom, he stopped. Then, he carefully put his foot down on the ground. He was the first man on the Moon.

Three hundred and twenty thousand kilometers away on Earth, people watched Neil Armstrong on television. They laughed and shouted. A man was on the Moon!

Jim Lovell sat in front of his television with his wife and children.

"I'm not the first man on the Moon," Jim said to his son Jeffrey. "But I will go there."

Jeffrey was only five years old and he was excited. "Look at the rocks, Dad!" he shouted. "Look at the moon rocks!"

"I see them, Jeffrey," Jim answered.

Jeffrey's sisters—Susan and Barbara—and his fifteen-year-old brother Jay watched, too. They saw a second astronaut, Buzz Aldrin, come out of the lunar module. He stopped at the top of the stairs, then he too climbed down to the Moon.

Jeffrey looked at his father. "Are you really going to the Moon?" he asked.

Jim smiled. "Yes, I am. But I went before, remember? I was on *Apollo 8*. We only went around the Moon on that trip—we didn't walk on it. But when I go on the *Apollo 14* trip, Fred Haise and I will walk on the Moon."

"When will you go?" asked Jeffrey.

"Neil Armstrong is on *Apollo 11*," said Jim. "Pete Conrad will go on the next trip. Alan Shepard will be on *Apollo 13*. After that, I'll go with *Apollo 14*."

"And will you bring me a moon rock?" Jeffrey asked.

Jim smiled. "I'll try."

"Really?" asked Jeffrey.

Jim put his arm around his son. "Yes," he answered. "I will bring you a moon rock."

Chapter 2   Thursday, April 2, 1970

Jim didn't have to wait for *Apollo 14*—the plans for the *Apollo* trips changed. Astronaut Alan Shepard had a problem with one of his ears and he couldn't go on *Apollo 13*. So Jim Lovell took his place.

"It's my time now," thought Jim. "I'm going to the Moon."

Jim wasn't the only astronaut on *Apollo 13*. The other men were Fred Haise and Ken Mattingly. Ken was the command module pilot and Fred was the lunar module pilot. They had important jobs. The command module was the *Apollo* astronauts' home for the long trip from Earth, and the small lunar module took the astronauts down to the Moon.

It was now nine days before the trip. The three astronauts were inside the command module simulator. They watched the controls in front of them.

"OK, Ken," said a controller at Mission Control. "You're the command module pilot. Can you dock *Odyssey* to *Aquarius*?"

"Yes, sir," answered Ken.

On the controls in front of him, there was an X and a picture of the lunar module. Ken had to get the X over the picture. That way, the lunar module and the command module could dock. This was important. The lunar module was behind the command module when *Apollo 13* left Earth. In space, the astronauts had to move it. They could only go from one module to the other module when the two modules were nose to nose.

Fred watched the numbers on the controls.

"Houston, we're at thirty meters now," he said into his radio.

The picture of *Aquarius* slowly moved close to the X.

"You're looking good," Mission Control said.

"We're at twenty meters, Houston," said Fred.

The mission controllers were in another room. One of them turned away from his radio.

"Let's make things difficult for him," he said to another man.

The other man smiled and pushed a control.

Suddenly, the lunar module on the controls moved quickly to the right.

"We have a problem," said Ken. He tried to move the picture of *Aquarius* back to the X. "I'm losing control."

"It's going to the right," said Fred Haise. "We're moving away." Ken tried again.

"No, now it's OK," he said. "We're OK."

Fred watched the numbers.

"Three meters," he said.

There was a noise.

"Houston, we did it!" Ken shouted.

"Good job!" said Mission Control. "You men are quick."

But Ken wasn't happy. "I want to do it again," he said.

Jim looked at him. "Again?"

"It has to be right," Ken answered. "I was slow. I don't want any problems in space."

Jim smiled. Ken always worked hard in the simulator. Sometimes Jim and Fred stayed and worked with him. But not tonight.

"I'm tired," said Jim. "And I'm a better pilot when I'm not tired. I'm going home to my family."

◆

Jim opened the door of his house and saw his wife, Marilyn.

"Jeffrey's waiting for you," she said. "He went to bed, but he has a lot of questions. I don't think he's asleep. Please go to him."

Jim went to Jeffrey's room. His son was on his bed. He always had a lot of questions. He wanted to know everything about Jim's job.

Jim sat on Jeffrey's bed.

"Tell me about the trip to the Moon, Dad," said Jeffrey.

Jim smiled. "OK," he said. "What do you want to know?"

"How long will it take?"

"Only four days," Jim answered. "First, a rocket will shoot us away from Earth. Then, when we're in space, some of the rocket engines will fall away from *Apollo*. We'll be close to the Moon after three days and the Moon's gravity will start to pull on us. We'll go around the Moon. Mr. Haise and I will get into the lunar module—we call it *Aquarius*. *Aquarius* will leave the command module *Odyssey* and carry us down to the Moon.

"Do you remember when Neil Armstrong walked on the Moon? Mr. Haise and I will walk on a new place, the Fra Mauro. There are some small mountains there so we'll have to be careful. After we get some rocks, we'll take some photos. Then we'll get back inside the lunar module and leave the Moon. Ken Mattingly will wait for us in the command module. We'll dock the two modules, and Mr. Haise and I will move back into the command module. Then Mr. Haise, Ken Mattingly, and I will fly back to Earth."

Jeffrey looked unhappy. "Can any of the machines break, Dad?" he asked.

Jim looked down at his son and smiled. "I don't think that will happen. Everything will be fine, and don't you forget it."

Jeffrey laughed. "I won't. But don't forget my moon rock."

Chapter 3   Thursday, April 9

Jim talked to a controller about *Apollo 13*. Near them, people worked on the Saturn rocket.

"They're getting it ready," said the controller. "In two days that rocket will take you into space."

A doctor came to Jim and the controller.

"I have to tell you something, Jim," he said.

"What is it?" asked Jim.

"One of the controllers has the measles."

"So?" said Jim. "The controllers aren't going with us."

"No," said the doctor. "But maybe you and the other astronauts will get it from him. Did you have the measles when you were a boy?"

Jim thought about it. "I don't remember," he answered. "Wait. Yes, I did!"

"Then you'll be OK."

Jim smiled. "Good. Then there's no problem."

"There *is* a problem," said the doctor. "Ken Mattingly didn't have the measles when he was young. We did some tests on him. We don't know that he won't get sick in space."

"But he's our command module pilot," said Jim. "He has to go. Fred and I worked with him in the simulator."

"I know," said the doctor. "I'm sorry."

Jim went to the mission controller's office. His boss was at his desk.

"The doctor says that Ken Mattingly can't fly with us," said Jim. "What does this mean?"

"What does it mean? You know the answer to that question. We have a big problem," answered his boss.

"But he *has* to go!" said Jim. "There are only two days before *Apollo 13* leaves. We can't go without Ken."

"Ken can't go," said his boss. "Jack Swigert will have to be the command module pilot."

Jim thought about Jack Swigert. He didn't know Jack as well as Ken.

"Jack Swigert is a good pilot," said the mission controller. "He can fly the command module, and he's ready."

"Yes, he's a good pilot," said Jim. "But he'll have to work in the simulator before we go. And now there's almost no time. Ken has to go."

"You can go with Jack Swigert, Jim, or you can stay here on Earth. There's no other way."

"But there are only two days before we go!"

Jim was very unhappy about Ken, but he wanted to go to the Moon.

"OK," he said. "Let's get Jack ready."

Chapter 4   Saturday, April 11

It was a beautiful warm Saturday in April at Cape Kennedy in Florida. The three astronauts looked up at the command module high on top of the 110-meter-high *Saturn 5* rocket. After long hard hours in the simulator, they were ready.

*The command module was high on top of the
110-meter-high* Saturn 5 *rocket.*

After long hard hours in the simulator, they were ready.

"When I went on *Apollo 8*," thought Jim, "the *Saturn 5* rocket did its job. That was my third trip into space. Now I'm going to do it again."

He looked at the other astronauts. This was their first trip into space. Were they afraid?

Jim thought about his first trip into space and smiled. "I was afraid," he remembered. "But I tried not to show it."

The three astronauts went up to the top of the rocket. Then, they got into the command module *Odyssey*. After the months in the simulator, they knew the command module well. Jim's chair was on the left. Jack's chair was in the middle and Fred's was on the right. In front of them were the controls—more than five hundred of them.

Outside the command module, a man closed the door. The astronauts watched the controls and waited.

At the big Mission Control room in Houston, Texas, the controllers were busy. They could see *Apollo 13* on their televisions.

"We're ready," said a controller.

"Ready," said a second man.

Their boss, Gene Kranz, listened. Then he spoke into his radio.

"Cape Kennedy, this is Houston. We're ready."

The people at Mission Control in Houston were excited. Only one man was quiet. Ken Mattingly stood away from the controllers and waited.

"OK, Houston," said a controller in Florida. "*Apollo 13* will go in one minute."

The time was 13:12.

Around the world, people sat in front of their televisions and waited. Inside the command module, the three astronauts waited too.

"Get ready, men!" Jim Lovell laughed. "It's time!"

"Twelve, eleven, ten, nine, eight, seven, six, five, four, three, two, one."

Suddenly, there was a loud noise. A long way below the astronauts, fire shot down from the engines of the *Saturn* rocket.

Jim Lovell smiled. "We're moving," he said.

People on the ground at Cape Kennedy looked up. The rocket was high in the Florida sky.

"Houston, they're going to the Moon," said the controller at Cape Kennedy.

"Thank you very much," Gene Kranz answered from Houston. "*Apollo 13* is ours now."

◆

Apollo 13 flew fast. Then the sound from the engines stopped. Below the command module, some rocket engines fell away.

"Get ready for a kick," said Jim.

Other rocket engines started and *Apollo* shot into space again.

"That was a big kick!" said Jack.

"Houston, the second engines started OK," said Jim.

Inside the command module, the three astronauts waited.

Below the command module, some rocket engines fell away.

"Thank you, *Apollo*," answered Mission Control. "Everything is fine."

Jim looked at the lights on the controls in front of him. There was one light for each of the rocket engines. Suddenly, the light in the center went out. It came back on, then went out again.

"This is *Odyssey*, Houston," Jim said into his radio. "We have a center engine light out. The other four engines are OK."

"Right, *13*," said Mission Control. "We have the same on our computer here."

Inside the command module, Jim and the other astronauts waited. They watched the controls, but the light in the middle didn't come on again. Jim looked at a different control.

"That control ends the trip and sends us back to Earth," thought Jim. "Will I have to push it?"

Jim closed his eyes and waited. He didn't want to go back to Earth—not now. He wanted to go to the Moon.

"Houston, what's the story on engine five?" he said into the radio.

"Engine five turned off early," said Gene Kranz.

"Do you know why?" asked Jim.

At Mission Control, Kranz looked at one of the controllers.

"Do we understand the problem?"

"No," said the controller. "But the other engines are OK."

"*Odyssey*, you don't have to come back," said Kranz. "The other engines are OK."

"Thank you, Houston," said Fred.

Jim looked at Fred and Jack. "Every space trip has a problem," he said with a smile. "And that was our problem for this trip."

Outside the command module, the sky was dark. *Apollo 13* was in space—160 kilometers above the Earth.

"*Apollo*, this is Houston. The rocket engines will turn off now. You'll go around the earth two or three times. We want to study our controls here."

"OK, Houston."

The engine noise stopped. It was very quiet. A notebook flew past the astronauts. Jim caught it in his hand.

"Gravity!" he said.

"You mean no gravity," laughed Fred. "Life is harder without it."

Outside, more rocket engines fell from *Apollo* and went away into space.

Jim looked out the window at the blue and green ocean below them. He picked up the camera and took a photo. Then *Apollo* turned and he could only see black space.

"OK," Jim said to the other astronauts. "Let's get *Apollo* ready for the trip to the Moon."

◆

The astronauts worked hard in the command module. Sometimes they stopped and took pictures of the Earth below them.

"We can see the sun coming up, Houston," said Jim. "We can see the Earth again. The colors look wonderful."

"It's beautiful," said Fred.

At Mission Control, Kranz watched *Apollo* on a map in front of him.

"That's their second trip around the Earth," he said to a controller. "Is everything OK in the command module?"

"Yes," answered the controller. "We can't find any problems. The engine will start in one minute. That will turn *Apollo* away from the Earth."

"*Apollo*, this is Houston," said Kranz. "Everything is OK. It's time for *Apollo*'s trip to the Moon."

Another engine started in the *Saturn* rocket and *Apollo* moved away from the Earth. Jim smiled. He felt great. He was in space again.

"OK," said Fred. "The Earth is behind us now. We can stop the engine."

One minute later the engine turned off, but *Apollo* didn't stop. It moved quickly through space.

"We're going to the Moon," laughed Jim.

"*Odyssey*, you have to dock with *Aquarius* now," said Mission Control.

Jim looked at Jack. "I hope he can do this," he thought.

Jack smiled. "I can do it," he said.

"I know," Jim answered.

Jack pushed a control with the letters CSM-SEP on it. The command module moved away from the rocket behind it. Slowly, it turned and the rocket was in front of *Odyssey*. Then the outside of the rocket fell away and there, inside, was the lunar module *Aquarius*. Jim saw its four legs.

"It's an animal," he thought.

"Two hundred meters," said Fred.

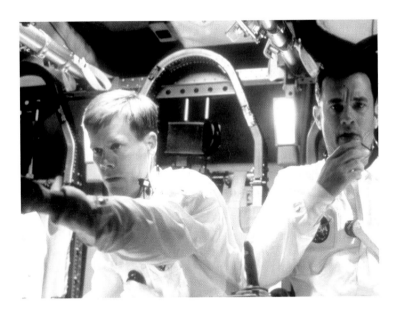

Jack pushed a control with the letters CSM-SEP on it.

Outside the window, the lunar module looked close now.
"One hundred meters."
Jack carefully moved the controls.
"It's almost there. Twenty meters."
Slowly, the lunar module and the command module met. There was a loud noise and the two modules docked. They were nose to nose in space.

"Houston, we have the lunar module," said Jim into his radio.
"OK, *Odyssey*," said Mission Control.
Jim looked at Jack. "Good job," he said.

Chapter 5   Monday, April 13, 20:24

"When's Dad coming on the television?" Jeffrey Lovell asked.
Jeffrey stood with his mother and sisters in Mission Control.

The other astronauts' families and friends were there, too. There was a big television in the room, but it had no picture on it.

"In a minute," his mother answered.

"Is he really going to talk to us from space?"

"Yes, he is."

Jeffrey was sorry about his brother Jay. Jay was away at school and couldn't be there.

"Do you think Dad's all right?" Jeffrey asked.

"He's fine," she answered. "Look around at the controllers. They don't look afraid. Everything is going to be fine."

"Dad said that too," said Jeffrey. "Wait! Look! There he is!"

The three *Apollo 13* astronauts were on the television. Jeffrey moved close to it and sat on the floor. He saw his father smile into the camera.

"Good evening, America," said Jim. "We're here in *Apollo 13*. We're talking to you from almost 320,000 kilometers away. Tonight, Fred Haise, Jack Swigert, and I will show you some of our little jobs out here in space.

"We have to eat so let's start with cooking. Cooking isn't easy without gravity. Things don't fall to the floor here."

Jeffrey saw his father take a bag in his hand.

"We carry bags of dry food," Jim said. "We put hot water in it before we eat it."

Then, Fred was on the television with Jim. He had a strange gun in his hand. Jim gave him the bag of food and moved away.

"Watch this!" Fred shouted. Water came out of the gun and went into the food bag. "Dinner! We don't really cook here in space."

Some water got out of the food bag and moved across the command module in front of Jack's nose. He played with it with his finger.

"Now," said Jim, "Fred and I will show you around the lunar module, *Aquarius*. After you, Fred."

"OK!" said Fred. He kicked his feet and moved through a small door.

"He's swimming," thought Jeffrey.

Jim went into the lunar module after Fred, then they turned to the television camera.

"This is *Aquarius*," said Fred. "The lunar module is very small— only as big as a closet. We only use it for the quick trip from the command module down to the Moon and back again. The walls of the lunar module are as thin as paper. Now, watch this."

He took a pen, a bag of food, and a light. Then he opened his hands. All three things turned around and around in front of his nose.

"That's my space game!" he laughed.

Fred and Jim moved back into the command module.

"We'll say goodbye now," said Jim. "Next time we'll be on the Moon. This is *Apollo 13*. Have a nice evening!"

"Don't forget my moon rock," Jeffrey called to the big television. He was happy now. His father was fine.

Chapter 6   Monday, April 13, 21:07

Jim turned off the television camera and closed his eyes. Everything was OK. It was April 13 on Earth. There were two more days before they got to the Moon.

"You were very good on television, *Odyssey*," said Mission Control on the radio.

Jack got into his chair.

"Thank you, Houston."

"Now, we have some little jobs for you," said Mission Control. "First, please change the controls on the oxygen tanks."

This helped the oxygen move through the command module and the machines. They had to have oxygen for the ship's power.

"OK," answered Jack. "I'll do that now."

Jack changed the controls.

Suddenly, there was a loud noise and Jim flew into a wall.

"WHAT WAS THAT?" he shouted.

Jack sat in his chair and watched papers and bags of food fly around inside the command module.

"What happened?" Jim asked again. He looked at the other astronauts, but they didn't answer.

Then there was a second loud noise.

"Look!" said Fred. "The lights on the controls are going crazy! I never saw that before!"

Jack spoke into the radio. "Houston, we have a problem."

"Say again," Mission Control answered.

"Houston, we have a problem."

Apollo moved strangely. It turned to the left and then quickly turned to the right. Things flew past the astronauts' heads.

At Mission Control, the controllers shouted. "Oxygen tank number two broke! There's no oxygen in it!"

"Number one broke, too!"

"I can't hear them on the radio!"

"One at a time," said Gene Kranz. He turned to one of the controllers. "Is this a problem with the controls? Or did a machine in the command module break?"

"My controls say that four machines broke in the command module," answered the controller. "But that's not possible! That can't happen!"

Three hundred and twenty thousand kilometers away, Jim looked around at the command module.

"Did a rock hit the lunar module?" he thought.

Astronauts were afraid of the smallest rocks in space. They were very dangerous.

Jim looked at Jack. "Close the door to the lunar module. Quick!" he shouted.

Jack moved to the door and pulled on it. The door didn't move.

"I can't close it!" he said.

"Forget it," said Jim. "The lunar module's OK."

"How do you know?" asked Jack.

"Because we aren't dead."

Jim moved to the window and looked out into space.

"We have another problem," he said.

"What do you see?" Fred asked.

"Look!"

Fred went to the window and looked out. "It's smoke!" he said. "Thin white smoke! It's coming out of the command module!"

Jack called Mission Control. "Houston, we can see smoke going out into space!"

"Wait," said Jim. "It's not smoke. I think it's oxygen! The oxygen is leaving the ship!"

Jim was right. There was no other answer.

"OK, *Odyssey*."

Jim looked at the controls.

"There's nothing in oxygen tank two," he said. "And not much in number one."

"We're not going to have any oxygen or any power," Fred said. "What can we do?"

At Mission Control, one of the controllers turned to Kranz.

"They have to turn off most of the machines in the command module," he said.

"What will that do?" asked Kranz.

"The machines are using power. Without power, the astronauts can't come home."

"But we can't turn off the machines," said Kranz. "The astronauts have to use every machine in the command module. They can't go to the Moon without them."

"They're not going to the Moon," said the controller. "*Odyssey* is dying."

Kranz looked at the controller. "Not go to the Moon? There has to be another way. Can we try something?"

"The astronauts will die without oxygen and power," said the controller. "We have to do something about that fast."

Kranz thought for a minute. "OK," he said. Then he spoke into his radio. "*Odyssey*, this is Houston. You're going to have to turn off some of the machines."

"Turn off some of the machines?" Jim asked. "Did I hear you right?"

"Yes, Jim," said Kranz. "The machines use a lot of power. That power is going to bring you home."

Jim couldn't speak. "We're not going to the Moon," he thought.

"Did you hear me, Jim?" Gene Kranz asked.

"We heard you, Houston," Jim answered.

He turned away from the radio and looked at Jack and Fred.

"We're not going to the Moon," he said.

Chapter 7   Monday, April 13, 22:35

Jim turned off some of the machines in the command module, then he looked out the window.

"Houston, this isn't helping," he said. "I can see oxygen outside. In two hours there will be no more oxygen."

They were a very long way from home. They had to do something—FAST. But what?

Suddenly, Jim had an idea—the lunar module! It was only for two men, and only for short trips. But it had power, and it had oxygen.

"We'll die inside the command module," he thought. "But we can go inside *Aquarius*. Then we can work with the problems in the command module."

At Mission Control, Gene Kranz and the controllers had the same idea.

"*Odyssey*," called Mission Control. "You men will have to leave the command module. You will have to go into the lunar module."

"OK, Houston."

"Start turning off all of the machines in the command module," said Mission Control. "At the same time, start the computer in the lunar module."

"I'll go into the lunar module now," said Fred. "I'll get it ready."

"How long will it take?" asked Jim.

Fred looked at his notes.

"About three hours."

"You will have to leave the command module in fifteen minutes," said Mission Control.

The notes fell out of Fred's hands, then moved near his head.

"Fifteen minutes!" thought Jim. "Fifteen minutes? That's not possible!"

Down on Earth, the Mission Control room was very busy. More and more controllers arrived from their homes.

Gene Kranz looked at them. "OK, controllers," he said. "We don't want these astronauts to die. We have to get them home. The computer in the command module is losing its power. We have to move everything to the lunar module computer, or they can't fly the ship. We don't have much time, so let's work fast!"

Chapter 8   Monday, April 13, 22:45

Fred and Jim were in the lunar module now. Jack was in *Odyssey*. In his hand was a book about the command module.

"We're losing power fast," he said into the radio. He quickly turned the pages. "Houston, do I look at the red pages?"

"Houston, I'm ready. I can turn on the lunar module computer now," Jim called from inside *Aquarius*.

"One at a time," said Mission Control. "For Jack, it's the red pages. For Jim, turn on controls eleven and thirty."

Jack studied the book, then he called out some numbers to the lunar module.

"OK, Jack," said Jim. "I'll work on those numbers."

The other astronauts waited.

"Ready, Jim?" asked Mission Control.

"In a minute."

"Turn off the power in *Odyssey*, Jack," said Mission Control.

"OK, Houston." Jack turned off the power.

But in the lunar module, Jim wasn't ready.

"Wait, Houston!" he said. "The computer isn't on in the lunar module."

Suddenly, *Apollo* had no power. The controls didn't work. The ship turned around and around in space.

"Houston, I can't control this thing!" Jim shouted. "The power is on now, but I can't work the controls!" He tried again. "The command module is pulling us. I can't turn the ship!"

"It's trying," said Fred.

"Trying what?" asked Jim.

"It's trying to stop turning."

Fred was right. Slowly, *Apollo* stopped turning.

"Houston, it's OK now," said Jim. "The controls in the lunar module are working. We're OK."

"That's good, *Aquarius*," said Mission Control. "Can you hear me, Jack?"

"Yes, Houston," Jack answered from the command module. It was dark in there now.

"Go into the lunar module now," said Mission Control.

"Houston, the machines are going to get very cold in here," said Jack. "Will they turn back on?"

Jack waited, but there was no answer. The radio was quiet. The lights were out. Slowly, Jack took one last look around *Odyssey*.

"We'll have to get home in this command module," he thought. "I hope it works."

Then, he turned and went into the lunar module.

Chapter 9   Monday, April 13, 23:00

Room 210 of Mission Control was full now. The controllers all talked about the problems of *Apollo 13*.

"Can we get the astronauts home?"

"How long can they live in the lunar module?"

"Will the engine on the command module work again?"

Then Gene Kranz came into the room and began to speak. The men were quiet.

"OK," said Kranz. "We have a problem. The astronauts are all in the lunar module. It has water, power, and oxygen for two men for two days. No more. Now there are three men in there. They will have to stay there for four or five days."

He waited, but his men were quiet.

"So let's think," said Kranz. "How do we get our people home?"

"We turn *Apollo* around," said a controller. "We turn it around and bring the astronauts home. We use the engine behind the command module and shoot them back to Earth."

"Wait," said Kranz. "That sounds dangerous. We don't know about that engine. Will it start again?"

"*Apollo* can go around the Moon," said a second controller. "That way we don't have to use that engine. We can turn them around with the Moon's gravity. Then, they can come back to Earth."

"Use the Moon's gravity?" said Kranz. "That will take three or four days. But it's the best idea."

"No! They don't have the time," said the first controller. "They can't live in the lunar module for four days."

The room was quiet.

"OK, let's think," said Kranz. "The command module has a problem. How bad is it? Does anybody know?"

Nobody spoke.

"The astronauts have to use the command module at the end of the trip. We know that," said Kranz. "But now they can only use the lunar module. They'll have to go around the Moon and then start the lunar module's engines. That's the quickest way."

"Those engines are for short trips!" said a controller. "They didn't build them for this!"

"Don't think about that," said Kranz. "This is the only possible way."

Chapter 10   Tuesday, April 14, 18:15

The astronauts heard the radio.

"*Odyssey*, it's time," said Mission Control.

"OK, Houston," said Jim.

"You'll be behind the Moon for twenty-eight minutes."

"OK, Houston."

This was Jim Lovell's second time behind the Moon. But this time was different. No conversation was possible with Mission Control behind the Moon and this trip was more dangerous.

The astronauts watched the Earth outside the window. It was small and blue. Then they were behind the Moon and they couldn't see it.

"Goodbye, Earth," Jack said quietly. "We'll see you again."

Suddenly, it was dark.

"The Moon is down there," Jim thought. "But we can't see it."

He thought about Neil Armstrong's feet on the Moon. Why Armstrong's feet? Why not his?

Then, suddenly, the Sun came up from behind the Moon. The astronauts saw gray mountains one hundred kilometers below them.

"Look down there," said Fred. "That place by the mountains— we planned to go there."

Jim thought about Jeffrey's moon rock. It was down there too.

"I'm sorry, Jeffrey," he said quietly. "Maybe next time."

Suddenly, the radio made a noise. They were around the Moon now.

"The Moon is down there," Jim thought.
"But we can't see it."

"*Apollo 13*, this is Houston," a controller said. "Hello, again."

"Hello, Houston," Fred said.

Now they could see the Earth outside the window.

"I think it's smiling at me," said Jack. He took a picture.

"It's time," said Jim. "Let's work. How much food and water do we have? Jack, get the water from *Odyssey* and bring it in here. It's going to get cold in the command module. We want water, not ice."

"OK," said Jack. He went into the command module.

Fred looked at some numbers in his notebook.

"We can start the lunar module's engines," he said. "But with them it's a three-and-a-half day trip back to Earth. We won't have much water."

"How much power do we have?" asked Jim.

"Not much."

Chapter 11   Tuesday, April 14, 20:40

At Mission Control a young controller, John Arthur, thought about the power on *Apollo*. He knew a lot about power.

John went to the front of room 210. Gene Kranz and some other controllers were there.

"The big problem is power," said John. "Without power they can't talk to us. Without power they can't control *Apollo*. Without power they can't get back to Earth at the end of the trip. We have to stop them using their power. They'll have to turn off their machines!"

"Which machines do they have to turn off?" asked Kranz.

"Almost all of them!"

"Almost all of them? They can't!"

"The lunar module will have no power in sixteen hours," said John.

"Don't we have fifty-five hours?" Kranz asked.

"No, we don't. We have sixteen hours of power. In sixteen hours, the men will die. We have to turn off almost everything in the lunar module. That's the only answer."

"But we can't do that!" said another controller.

"We have to," said John. "We have to turn off the computer, the lights, the controls!"

"But then they can't control *Apollo*!" said a second controller. "How will they get home?"

"Listen," said John. "We don't have time for this. They're using their power right now!"

"OK," said Kranz. "First, we use the engines and turn them away from the Moon. Then, we turn off the power in the lunar module. When they get close to the Earth, they'll have to turn the machines on again in the command module."

"The machines will be very cold," said a controller. "Will they start again?"

"They'll have to," said Kranz. "We'll work on the problems in the simulator. I want every controller to work on this. We have to have answers! How much power does the computer use? How much power do the lights use? Everything. We have to think about every machine in that ship!"

Up in space, the astronauts were ready.

"OK, men," said Jim. "We have to turn *Apollo* away from the Moon. Let's do this right. We don't want to stay in space."

He looked at the other astronauts and pushed a control. The lunar module's little engines came on.

"Houston, the engines are OK," said Jim. "We're coming back to Earth."

The astronauts looked out the window and watched the Moon. It slowly got smaller. They were on their way—to somewhere.

Chapter 12   Tuesday, April 14, 23:00

People all over the world knew about *Apollo 13* now. They read about it in newspapers and watched pictures of Mission Control on television. They all wanted the astronauts to come home. Ken Mattingly wanted them home, too.

The doctors were wrong about Ken—he didn't get the measles. When he walked into the simulator building in Houston, the controllers were happy. Ken knew more about *Apollo 13* than they did.

"Ken! This is great!" said John Arthur. "We want you in the simulator."

"How much power does *Apollo* have?" Ken asked. "Do we know?"

"No, not really," John answered.

"OK," said Ken. "Let's find the astronauts more power. The command module is cold now, so make the simulator cold. Everything in the simulator has to be the same. Give me a light."

A controller gave Ken a light. Ken gave it back.

"They have a different kind of light up there," he said. "I only want the same."

Ken took a book and went into the simulator.

Above him in space, the astronauts started to turn off their machines and their engines. Gravity threw them to Earth. Ken didn't have much time.

Chapter 13   Wednesday, April 15, 1:30

There were beds now in the rooms at Mission Control. Some of the tired controllers were asleep in them. Other men studied books and plans.

In space, the astronauts were tired too. They were also cold and wet.

26

Jack was in the dark command module. He wrote some numbers down.

"Something isn't right," he thought. He studied the numbers again, then went into the lunar module.

"Look at the numbers," he said to the other astronauts. "We're going to fly past the Earth. Then we'll start to move around the Sun."

Jim and Fred looked at him.

"How do you know?" asked Fred. He didn't feel well. He was very cold, but his head was hot.

"I know!" Jack said. He sounded angry.

"The Mission Control men are working on the numbers too," said Jim. "They're smart men."

"I think they made a mistake."

"Then they'll tell us about it."

"I don't think they will," said Jack. "They're not going to tell us about their mistakes."

"That's crazy," shouted Fred.

"Listen, I only changed the oxygen controls," Jack said. "And what happened? Everything broke."

"Did you read the controls before you changed them?" asked Fred.

Jack looked at him angrily.

"Don't tell me about *Odyssey*. I can fly this ship. Mission Control said, 'Change the controls,' so I did. I did my job!"

"It's OK, Jack," said Jim. "You didn't make a mistake. I know that."

"So, tell Fred!"

Chapter 14   Thursday, April 16, 04:14

The astronauts were tired and cold. The lunar module was dirty. There was no gravity so food, papers, and other things moved by their heads.

"Did you read the controls before you changed them?" asked Fred.

"Hello, *Apollo*," said the radio. "This is Mission Control. The doctor wants you to sleep now."

Jim moved in his chair.

"We're trying to sleep," he said angrily. "But it's very cold!"

At Mission Control, Gene Kranz looked at his controls. Something wasn't right.

"Are they going the right way?" he asked a controller.

"No, there's a problem," the man answered.

"What is it?" asked Kranz.

"They'll come close to Earth and then go out into space again. They have to turn *Apollo*. They have to start the engines."

"Can they start the engines again?" Kranz asked. "Do they have the power for that?"

"I hope they do," answered the controller. "We want them to come home."

In *Apollo*, Fred was sick. The astronauts were all thirsty and there wasn't much water now.

Jim heard the radio. "*Aquarius*, you're not coming to Earth," said Mission Control. "You have to start the engines."

"We'll have to start the computer," Jim said.

"Sorry, Jim," Mission Control answered. "You don't have the power for that."

"What?" said Fred. "We're doing it without the computer?"

"There's no other way," said Mission Control.

"OK," said Jim. "We're ready."

Suddenly, Jim felt good. Computers always flew *Aquarius* for him. But he was a pilot—now he wanted to fly his ship.

"OK, men," he said. "We can't use the computer, so let's fly this thing. All three of us will have to work. Jack, you watch the clock. The time is very important. Also, watch the Earth through the window. We're going that way."

"OK," said Jack.

"Fred, can you help me?" asked Jim.

"OK," said Fred. He tried to sound strong.

"Start the engines when you're ready," said Mission Control.

Jack looked at his watch. "Four, three, two, one . . . !"

"Now!" said Jim, and he pushed the controls.

They felt the engines turn on. Then *Apollo* started moving strangely. Jim fought with the controls.

"It's turning to the left!" Jack shouted.

Fred helped Jim with the controls.

"We'll be OK," he said.

"I can't see the Earth," said Jim. "Where is it? Where is it?"

Jack looked out the window. Where was it?

"Fred, can you see Earth?"

"There!" Fred answered. "Turn a little to the left."

Jim looked out the window. Where was it? Wait! There it was!

Jim looked at the Earth. It was beautiful. He turned the ship, then pushed a red stop control. It turned off the lunar module's engines.

"We turned off the engines, Houston," said Jim. "I hope we don't have to do that again."

"OK," said Houston.

On Earth, Ken Mattingly was in the simulator.

"How will they come back to Earth?" he thought.

He spoke to John Arthur on the simulator radio. "Put on the power for the controls and the radio," he said. "Then, for the parachutes and the command module engines."

"They won't have the power for the engines and the parachutes," said John.

"They're going to go down on the ocean," said Ken. "They have to use parachutes. And they have to use the engines too."

"You're asking me for everything, but that's not possible," said John. "We don't have much power."

"OK," said Ken. "Let's find more power. There has to be an answer. Let's start again. Let's get busy!"

Chapter 15   Friday, April 17, 5:14

Inside the lunar module, Jim watched Fred.

"He's getting weaker," he thought. "We have to get him home!"

Jim spoke into the radio. "Houston, what are we going to do when we get close to Earth? What's your plan?"

"We'll tell you the plan, *Aquarius*," answered Mission Control, "but not now."

Jim looked at Jack. "Do they have a plan?"

"I don't think they do," Jack answered. "They're trying to find one."

"I think Jack's right," said Fred weakly.

"Listen, Houston," said Jim into the radio. "We can't wait. We're very tired. Fred is sick. We can't think very well, so give us a plan. We have to be ready. We don't want to make any mistakes!"

"Ken Mattingly is working on the problem in the simulator right now, Jim," said Mission Control.

"Ken's working on it?" Jim said. "He doesn't have the measles?"

This was good—very good. Ken was the best man for the job.

At Mission Control, Ken spoke to John Arthur on the simulator radio.

"We have to think about this another way," he said. "We know there's some power in the lunar module, right?"

"Yes, a little," John answered.

"That's it! They can move that power to the command module. Then, they can start the machines in the command module and come home!"

Ken and John tried it in the simulator.

"Are the numbers OK?" asked Ken.

"They're fine," John answered. "Don't stop."

"Now I'll turn on the computer."

"Is your computer on?" asked John.

"Yes! What do you think?"

"They're going to be OK!" said John. "We found more power for the astronauts!"

Ken quickly climbed out of the simulator and ran into the Mission Control room. He spoke into a radio.

"*Aquarius*," he said, "this is Houston. Can you hear me?"

"We can hear you," answered Jim. "You don't have the measles!"

Ken laughed. "No Jim, I'm fine. Is Jack in the lunar module with you?"

"I'm here," said Jack.

"Jack, this is Ken Mattingly. Go into the command module and find some paper—a lot of paper."

When Jack was ready, Ken told him his plan. Jack wrote it down. There were a lot of numbers. After a week in space and days without sleep, Jack was very tired. He closed his eyes for a minute, then opened them again.

"Houston, wait," he said. "I can't read my numbers very well."

"That's OK," said Ken. "I'll tell you the plan again slowly."

Jack looked around at the command module. It was dark and cold. "The controls are wet," he said. "Will they work?"

"They'll be OK," said Ken.

Jack closed his eyes again. Then he opened them and started work. A light turned on—it worked. Jack pushed the different controls. Slowly, the lights and machines in the command module turned on.

"Are they OK?" asked Ken.

"Yes, the controls are all on, Ken!" Jack laughed. "They're all working!"

"*Apollo*, there's one more thing," Ken called to the other astronauts in the lunar module. "You have to move some heavy things into the command module."

"Why?"

"There are no moon rocks in the command module. It's too light."

"Right, Houston," said Jim sadly. He and Fred threw books, clothes, the TV camera, everything into the command module. But Jim thought about Jeffrey and his moon rock.

Chapter 16   Friday, April 17, 10:43

Jim looked around *Aquarius*. Now they had to go into the command module.

In front of them, the Earth was a large blue ball.

"Let's go, Fred," said Jim.

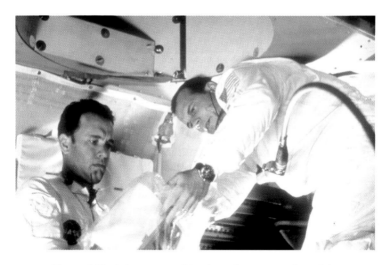

Jim and Fred threw everything into the command module.

Fred looked very sick. His face was a gray color, and he was very cold.

"You don't look well," said Jim.

"Forget it," Fred said. "I'm OK."

"Can you wait two or three more hours?" asked Jim.

"Yes. I have to."

"When we parachute into the South Pacific Ocean, it's going to be nice and warm."

Fred thought about the warm weather and smiled.

"Why don't you go help Jack?" said Jim. "I'll finish things in here."

"OK," said Fred.

Jim watched him move slowly into the command module.

"Jim," Jack called from the command module. "It's almost time. Come through now."

Ken was on the radio again.

"*Apollo*, the lunar module will leave the command module in one minute. Is everybody in *Odyssey*?"

Jim moved quickly from the lunar module into the command module. He closed the door.

"Jim?" shouted Jack.

"I'm here," said Jim. He went to the left chair—the pilot's chair. But Jack was there.

"Sorry," said Jim. He smiled. "I forgot. This is your ship now. Fly us home."

"Thanks."

Jack pushed a control and the lunar module moved away from the command module. The astronauts looked out the window and watched it move into black space. They were almost sad.

"Goodbye, *Aquarius*," the astronauts called quietly. "We thank you."

Jack looked at the controls. He thought about the engines and the best way down to Earth.

"We're coming home, Houston," he said.

"OK, *Odyssey*," Houston answered. "We're waiting for you."

At Mission Control, one controller didn't have a smile on his face.

"Look," he said to Gene Kranz. "They didn't turn right."

"It was almost right," said Kranz. "We can't help them now."

"Are you going to tell them?"

"No," said Kranz. "They don't have to know. Now we can only wait and hope."

Chapter 17 Friday, April 17, 11:53

Gravity pulled the command module. The astronauts were almost home, but they couldn't see the Earth below them. The nose of the command module was at the back. They had to come in that way so the nose of the command module didn't get really hot.

The command module fell quickly.

"You're looking good, *Odyssey*," said Mission Control. "We'll

34

talk to you again when your parachutes open in three minutes."

The three astronauts watched the window. The black sky changed to blue, red, and orange—the color of fire. The outside of the command module was very, very hot.

The astronauts closed their eyes.

Everybody at Mission Control watched a big television. Nothing came from the radio.

"Do you know anything?" asked Ken Mattingly.

"Nothing," said a controller.

"Can the people on the *Iwo Jima* see them?"

The *Iwo Jima*, a big ship, was in the Pacific Ocean. The men on the ship watched the sky.

"No," said a controller. "They can't see the command module."

Around the world, people watched their televisions and waited.

Small airplanes flew from the *Iwo Jima*.

Ken spoke into his radio. "*Odyssey*, this is Houston. *Odyssey*, can you hear me?"

There was no answer.

"Where ARE they?" shouted a controller.

"*Odyssey*, this is Houston," Ken called. "Four minutes, *Odyssey*. Can you hear us?"

The world waited, but the radio was quiet.

A man in an airplane looked at the sky through his camera.

"What's that?" he asked.

It was *Odyssey*. Big, orange parachutes opened in the sky. Slowly, the command module came down. Then, it was on the ocean—a small gray boat.

Chapter 18   Friday, April 17, 12:07

Jim Lovell's family was in front of their television with the other astronauts' families. It was a long wait.

"We can see *Odyssey*," said the man on the television happily. "The astronauts are back on Earth!"

The Lovell house went crazy. Jim's wife put her head in her hands and cried. The families of the other astronauts jumped up and down. But Jeffrey didn't move.

"My father is OK," he thought. "My father's coming home. My moon rock isn't important. He's coming home!"

Inside the command module, the astronauts smiled.

"Hello, Houston," Jim said into the radio. "This is *Odyssey*."

"Hello, *Odyssey*," Ken answered.

Odyssey moved slowly on the ocean. The orange parachutes were in the water now, too. The astronauts were quiet. They listened for the sound of an airplane. When they heard it, they smiled. They closed their eyes. They were OK. Now they only had to wait for the men from the *Iwo Jima*.

The door opened and the three astronauts walked out.

They were very tired and Fred was very sick. Jack's arms and legs hurt. But they were OK.

Then the men from the *Iwo Jima* opened the command module door. Through the door, the astronauts saw the blue Pacific Ocean. One of the men from the airplane helped Fred out the door.

"You're home," said the man.

Jim watched the men help Fred and Jack into the airplane.

"It was a good trip," he thought. "We didn't walk on the Moon, but we're back. That's the important thing. We're back."

Five minutes later, Jim was in the airplane with Jack and Fred. He looked down at the wonderful blue ocean and smiled.

The airplane flew to the *Iwo Jima*. The door opened and the three astronauts walked out.

ACTIVITIES

Chapters 1–5

Before you read

1 The men on *Apollo 13* didn't walk on the Moon, but *Apollo 13* is famous. Why?

2 Find these words in your dictionary. They are all in the story.

  astronaut   Earth   engine   Moon   pilot   rocket   simulator
  space

  Which are words for:

  a people?

  b machines?

  c places?

3 Look at the sentences. Find the words in *italics* in your dictionary. Then put these words in the sentences:

  airplane   rocket   spaceship   astronauts   ground   meet   sick

  a A . . . . . takes the *command module* and the *lunar module* into space.

  b Pilots use *controls* when they fly an . . . . . .

  c When a spaceship *docks* at a space station, they . . . . . in space.

  d Our feet stay on the . . . . . because of *gravity*.

  e When you have the *measles*, you feel . . . . . .

  f *Mission Control* in Houston talks to . . . . . in their spaceship.

  g Astronauts take *rocks* from the Moon home in their . . . . . .

After you read

4 Discuss these questions.

  a Why doesn't Ken Mattingly go on *Apollo 13*? Why is this a possible problem?

  b What problem does *Apollo 13* have when it leaves the Earth? Is this important?

5 You are Jim Lovell's wife or one of his children. How did you feel before Jim left? How do you feel now? Why?

Chapters 6–10

Before you read

6 Look at the picture on page 23. What do you think the astronauts are looking at?

7 Find the words in *italics* in your dictionary. Why are *tanks* of *oxygen* and *power* very important on a spaceship?

After you read

8 Who says these things?
   a "Houston, we have a problem."
   b "We're not going to the Moon."
   c "We don't want these astronauts to die. We have to get them home."
   d "Houston, the machines are going to get very cold in here. Will they turn back on?"

9 Work with another student. Have this conversation.
   Student A: You are Jim Lovell. You are in the command module. Something is wrong. Tell Mission Control.
   Student B: You are Gene Kranz at Mission Control. Ask Jim questions. What happened? What did he hear? What can he see?

Chapters 11–18

Before you read

10 Do the astronauts come home? How? What do you think?

11 Find the word *parachute* in your dictionary. Why do you think parachutes are important to the astronauts on *Apollo 13*?

After you read

12 Answer these questions.
   a How do Ken and John find power for the astronauts?
   b Why can't the astronauts see Earth at the end of their trip?
   c When Gene Kranz finds a new problem with the spaceship, he doesn't tell the astronauts. Do you think this is right? Why (not)?

Writing

13 You work for a newspaper. Write a story about *Apollo 13*. Why didn't the astronauts walk on the Moon? How did they get home?

14 You are an astronaut on *Apollo 13*. You have a TV camera, and people on Earth are going to watch you on television. What are you going to show them?

15 You are Gene Kranz. Write a letter to your mother after the astronauts are home. How did you feel when you were in Mission Control? Why? How do you feel now?

16 Do you want to go to the Moon? Why (not)? Write about it.

Answers for the Activities in this book are published in our free resource packs for teachers, the Penguin Readers Factsheets, or available on a separate sheet. Please write to your local Pearson Education office or to: Marketing Department, Penguin Longman Publishing, 5 Bentinck Street, London W1M 5RN.

BESTSELLING
PENGUIN READERS

AT LEVEL 2

American Life

Audrey Hepburn

Black Beauty

The Call of the Wild

A Christmas Carol

The Last of the Mohicans

Mr Bean

The Railway Children

The Secret Garden

Treasure Island

Walkabout

White Fang